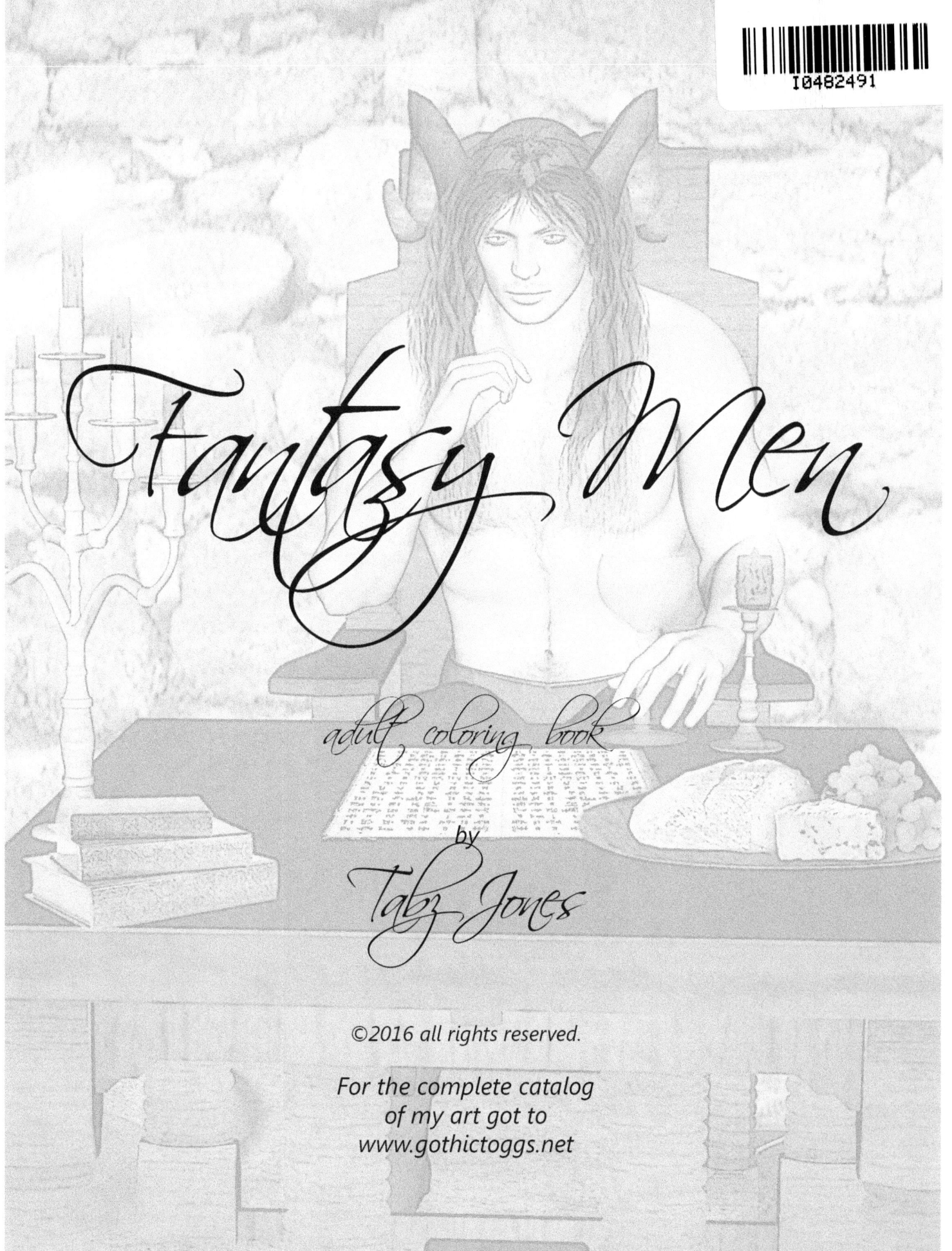

Fantasy Men

adult coloring book

by

Tabz Jones

For the complete catalog
of my art got to
www.gothictoggs.net

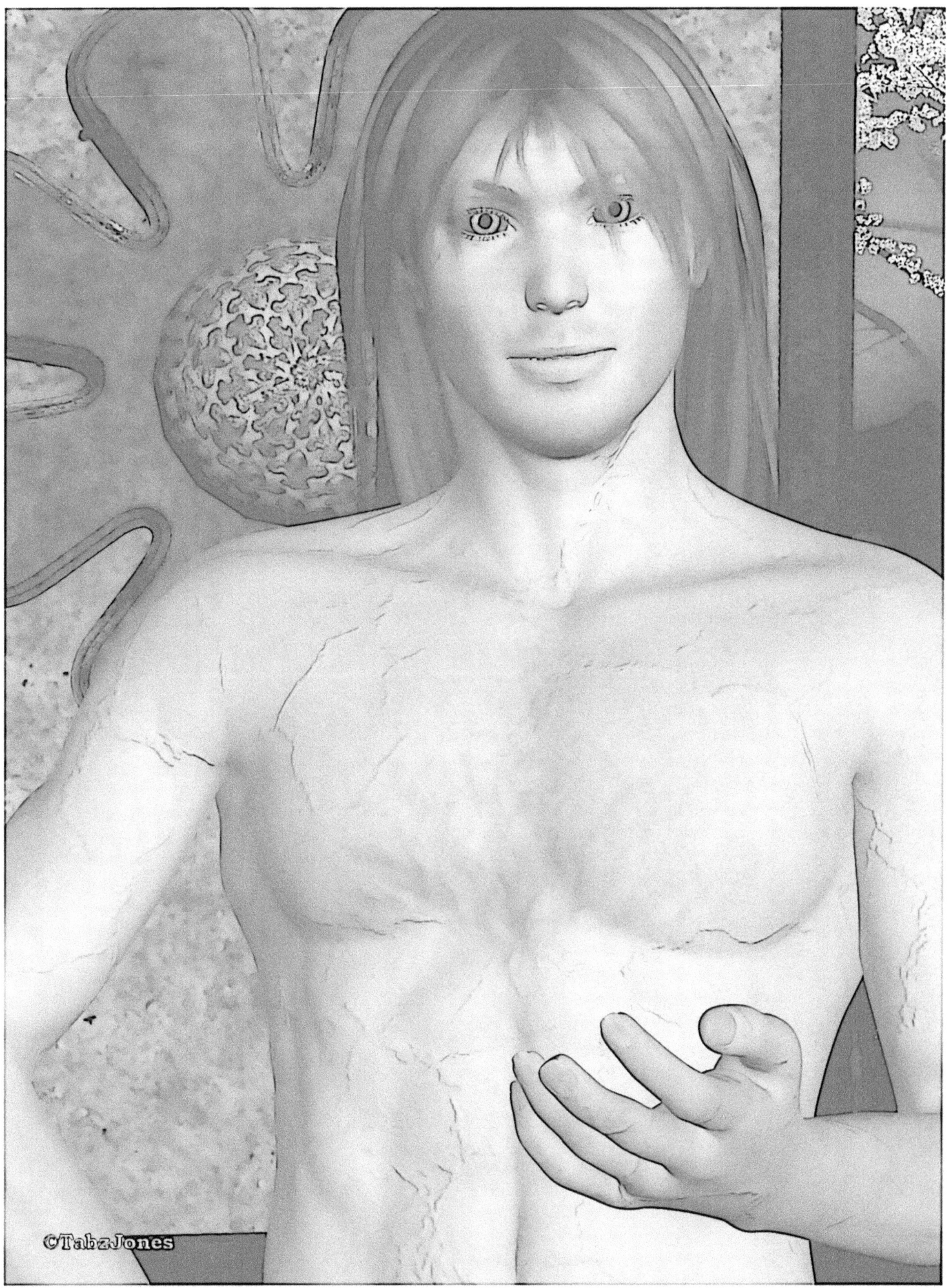

©TabzJones

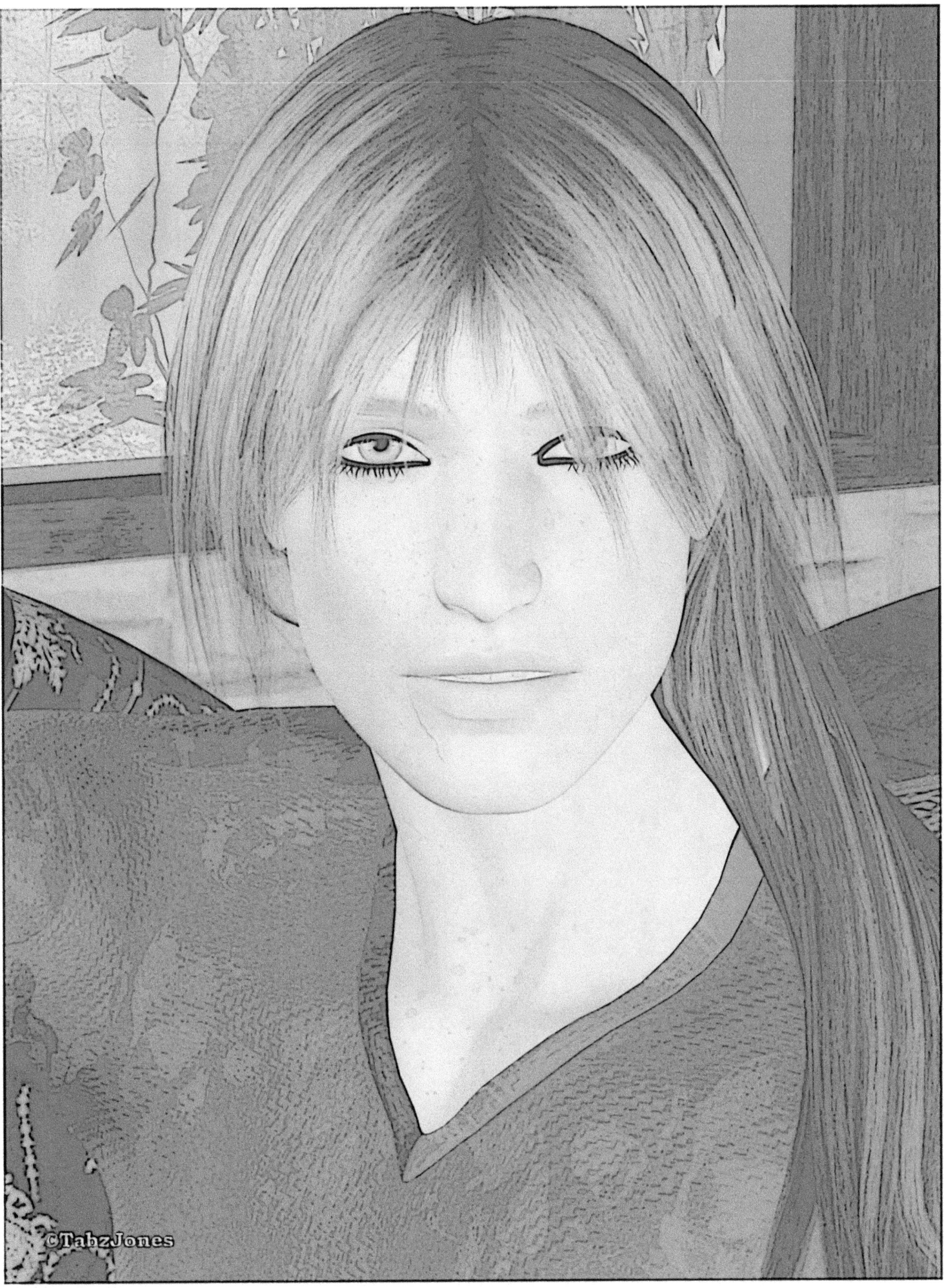

©TabzJones

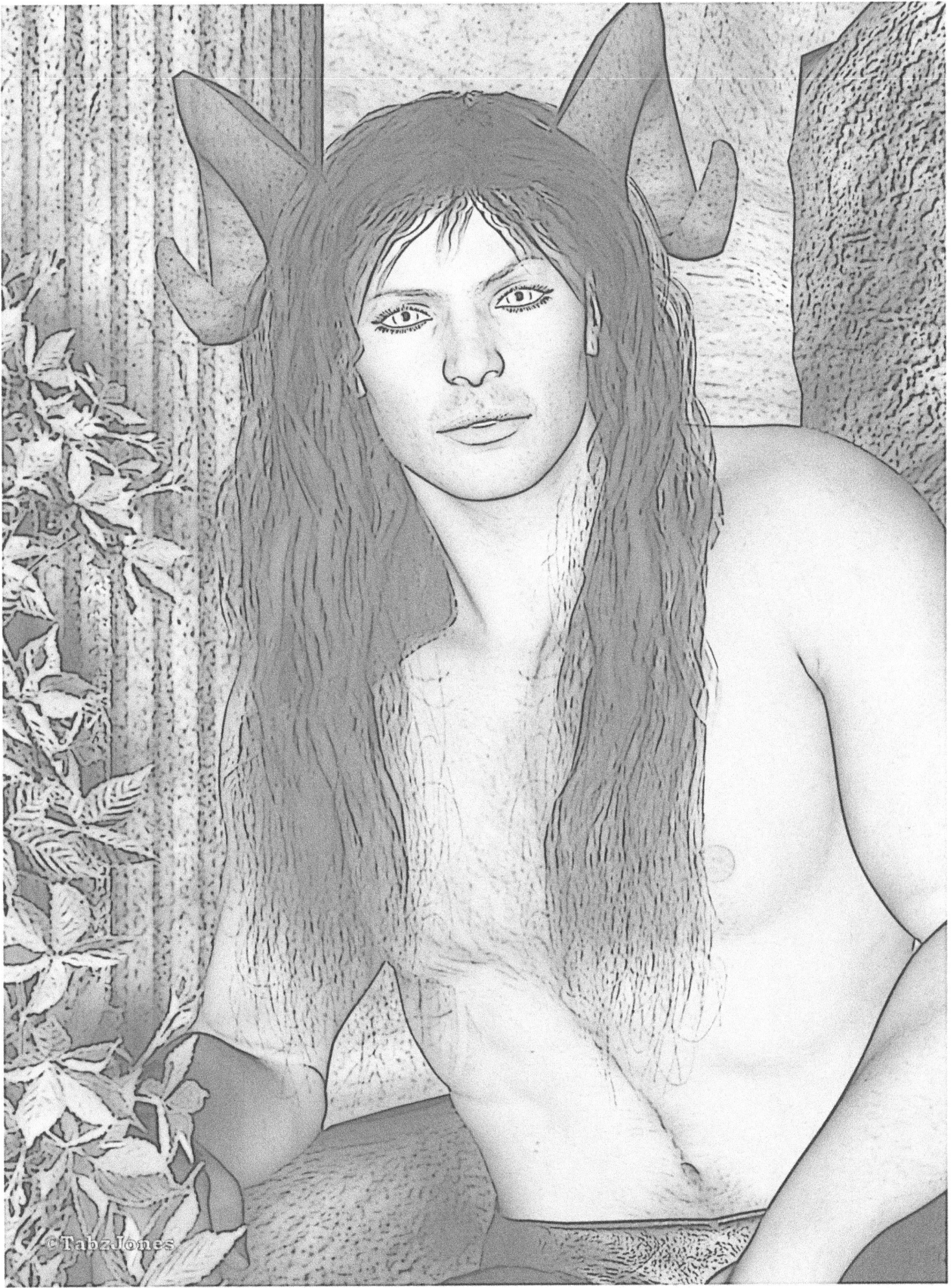
© TabzJones

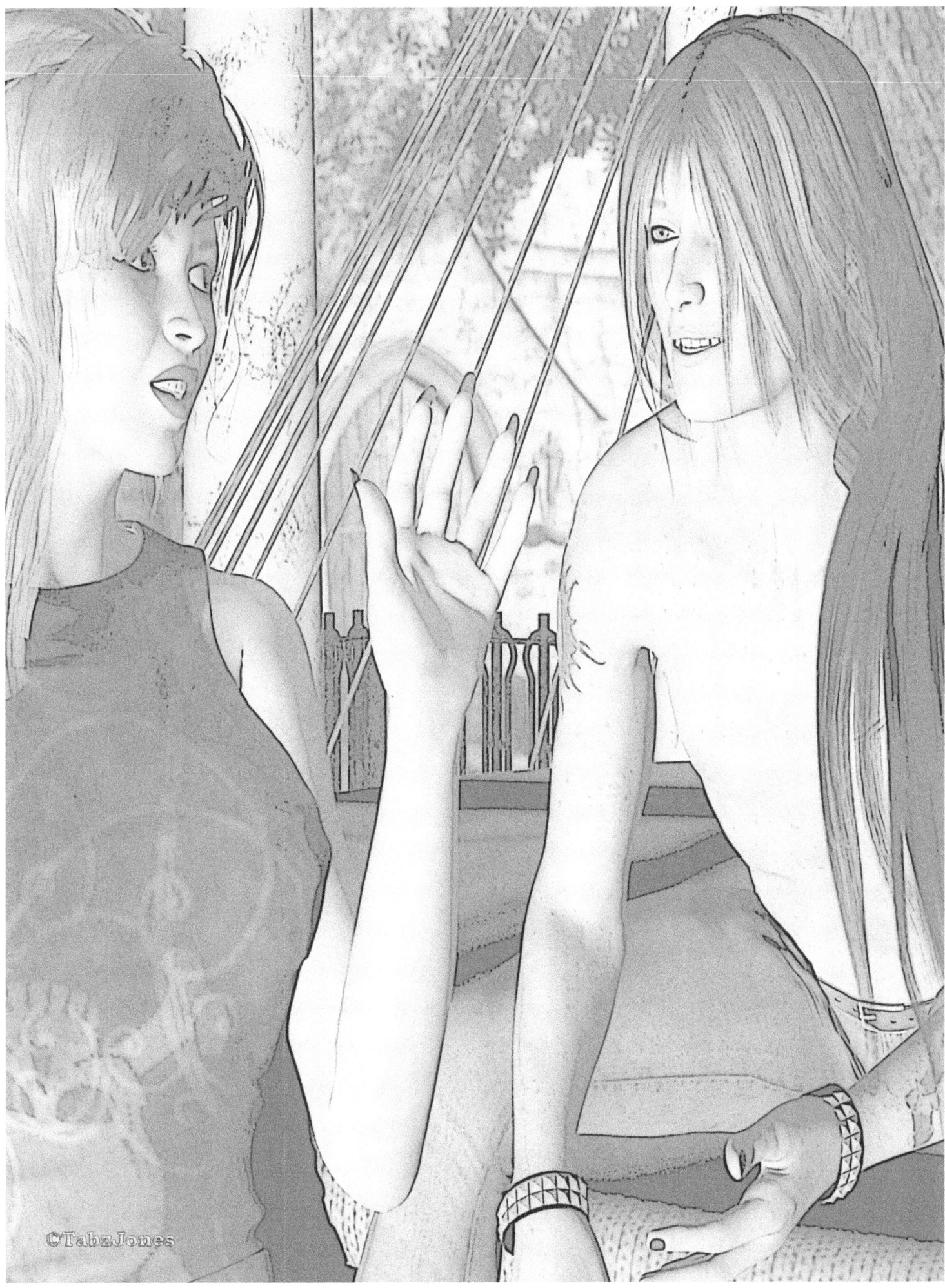

©TabzJones

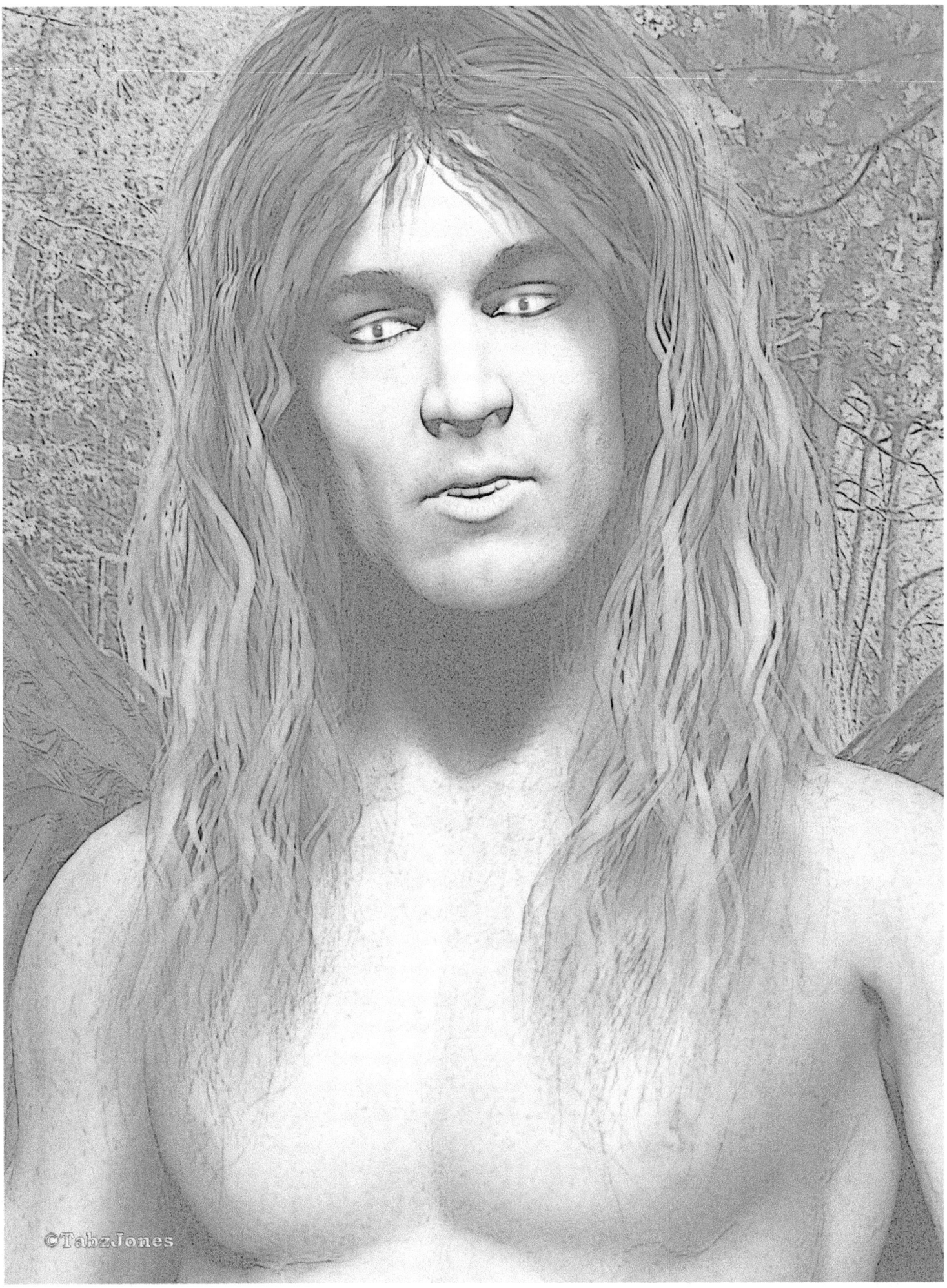
©TabzJones

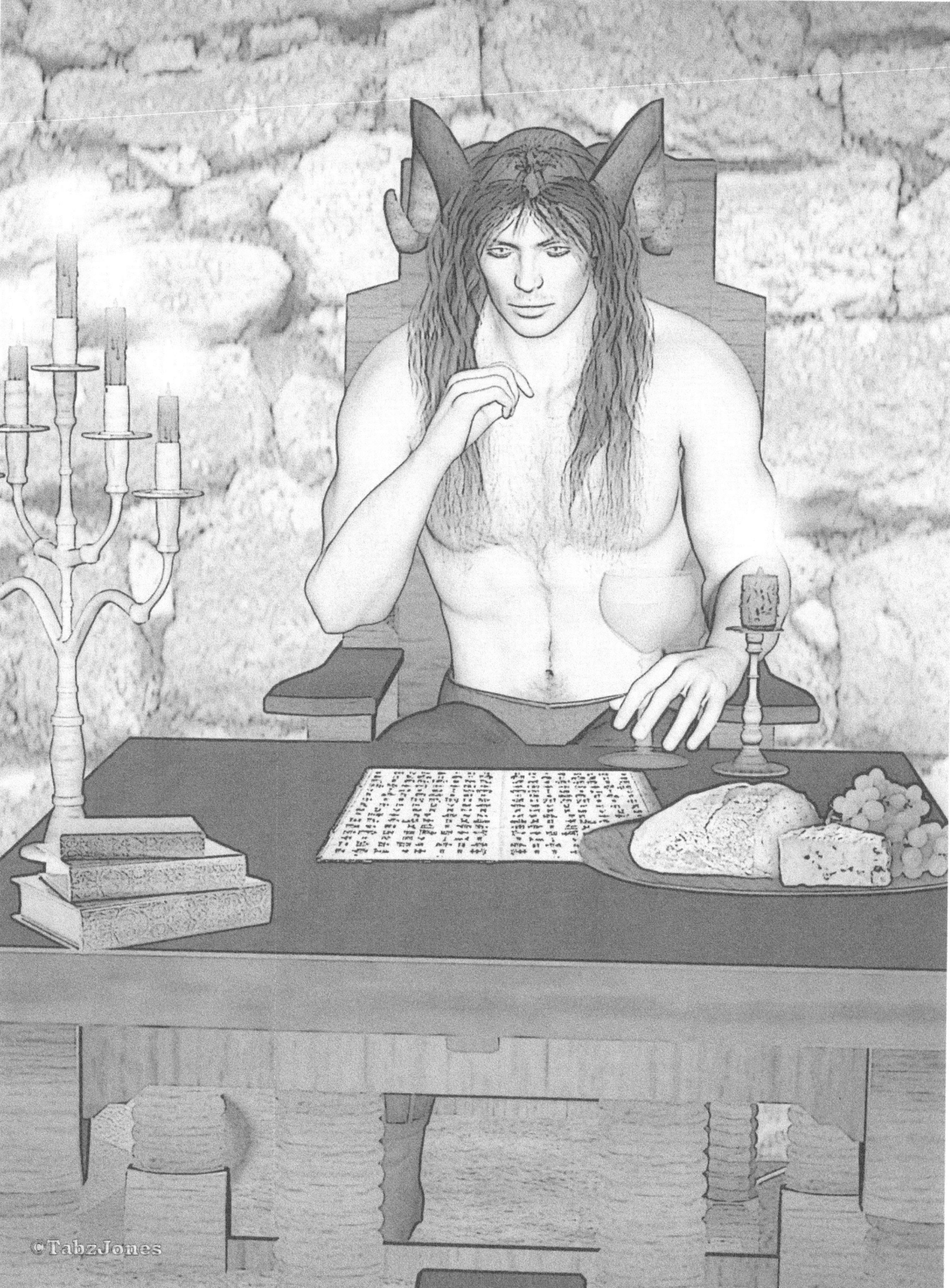

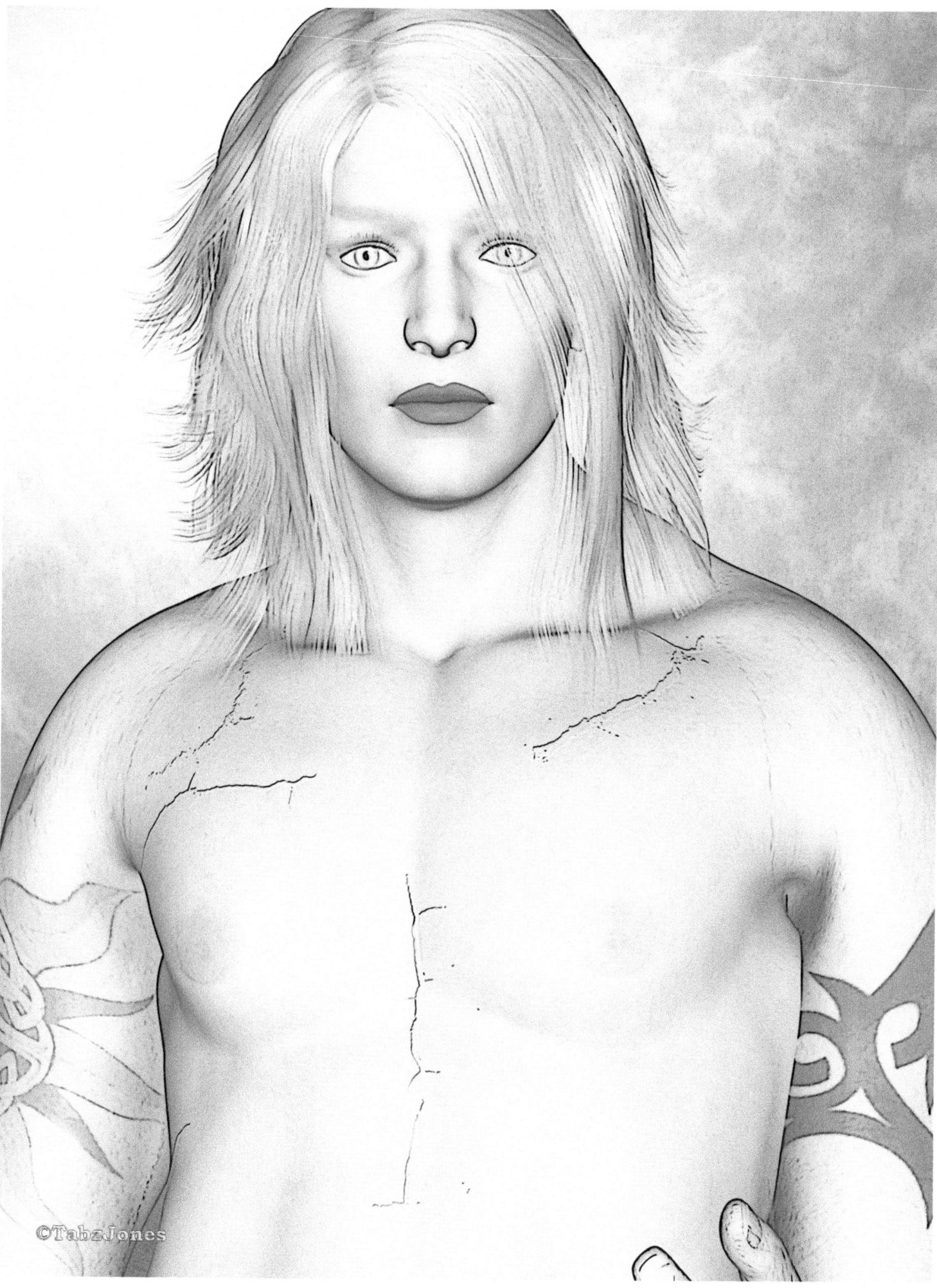

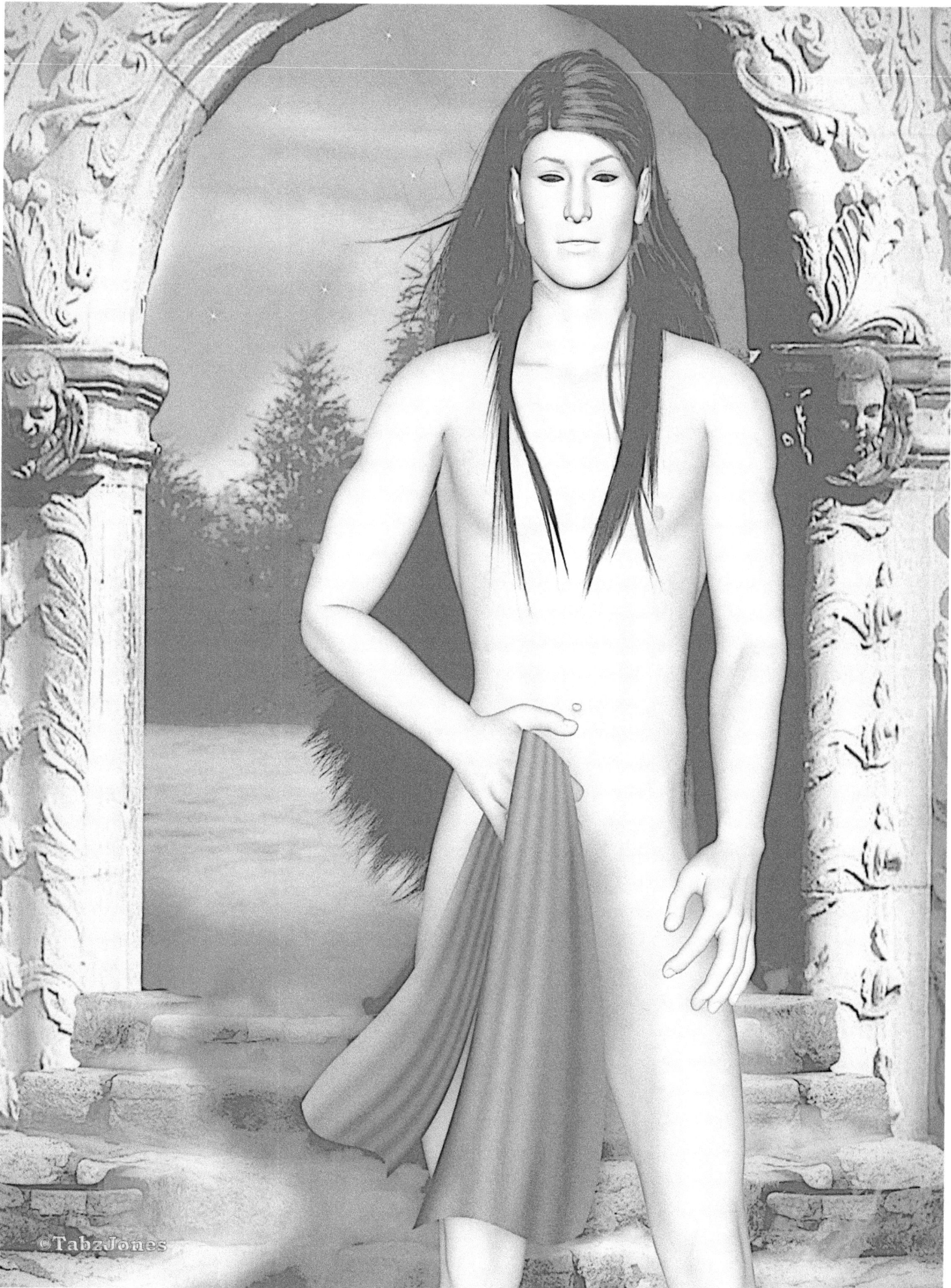

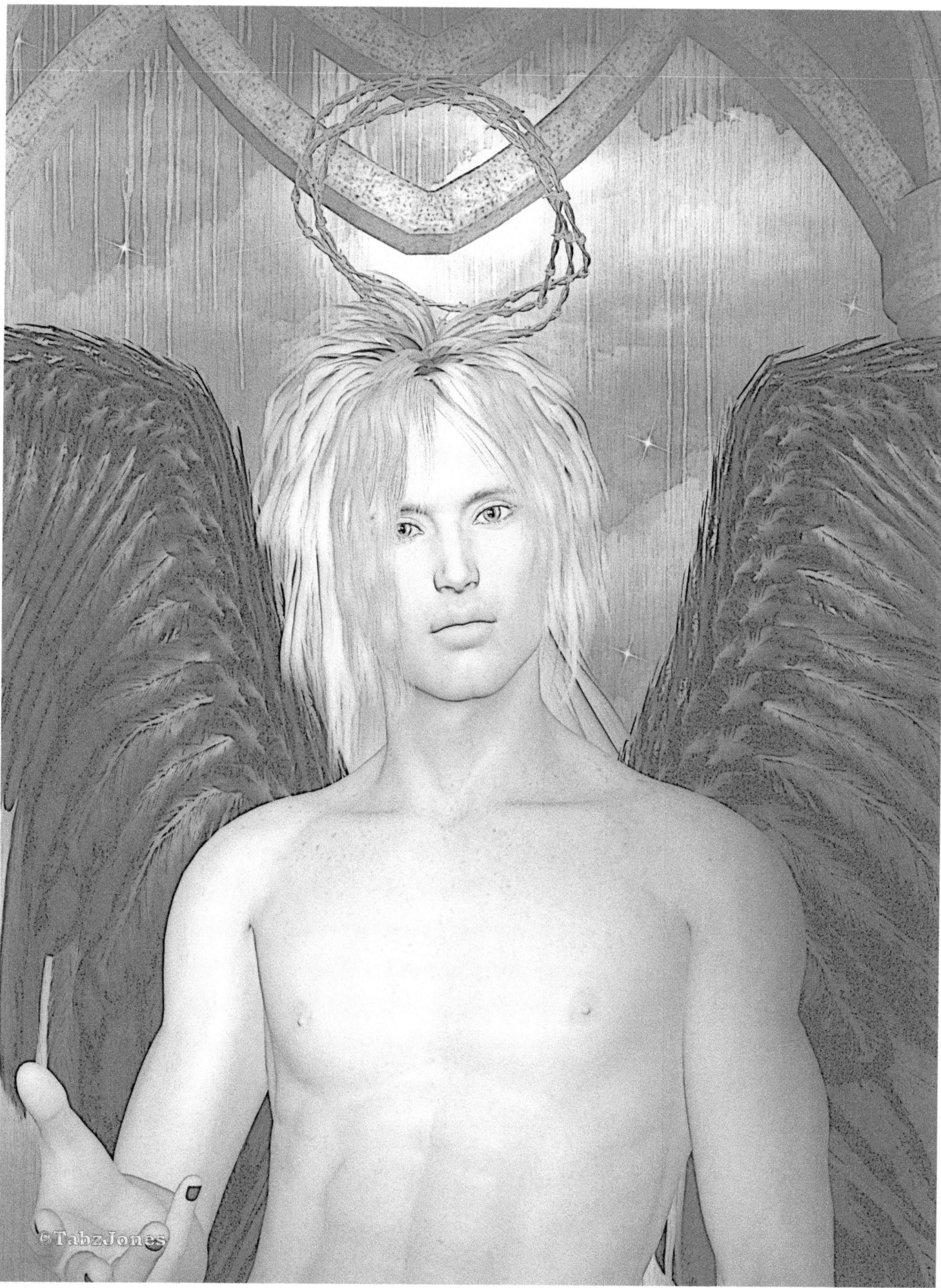
©TabzJones

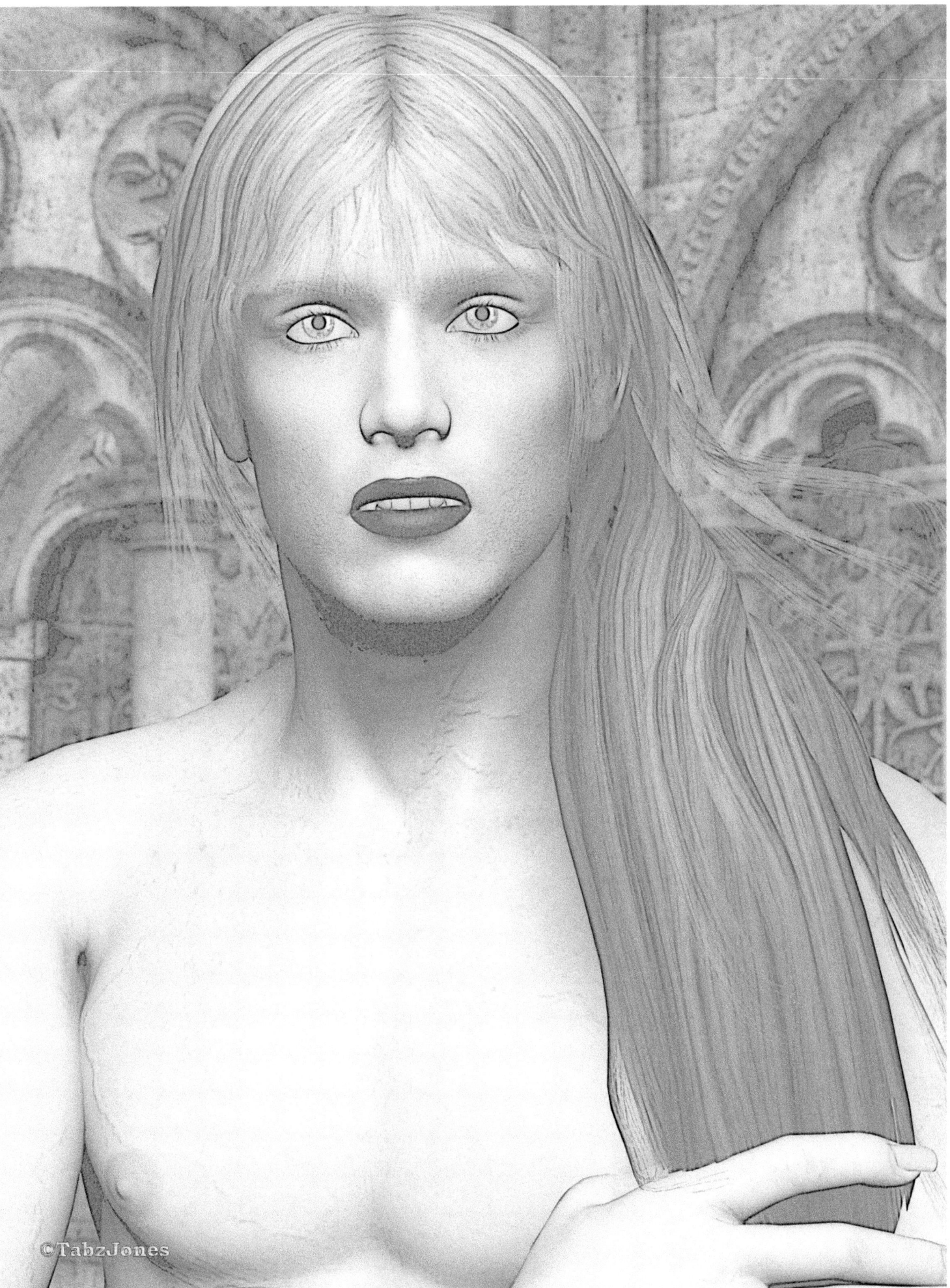

©TabzJones

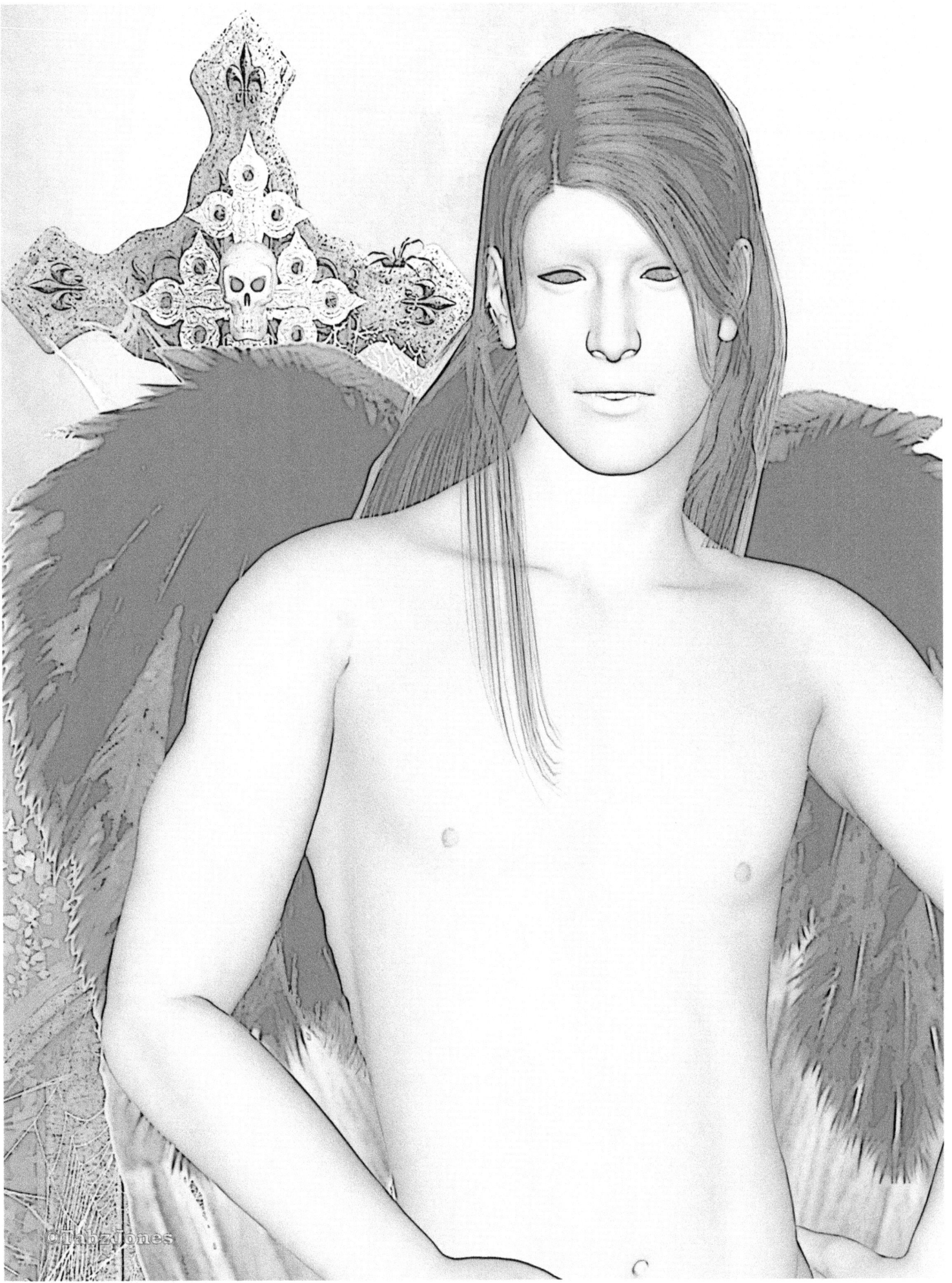

©TabzJones

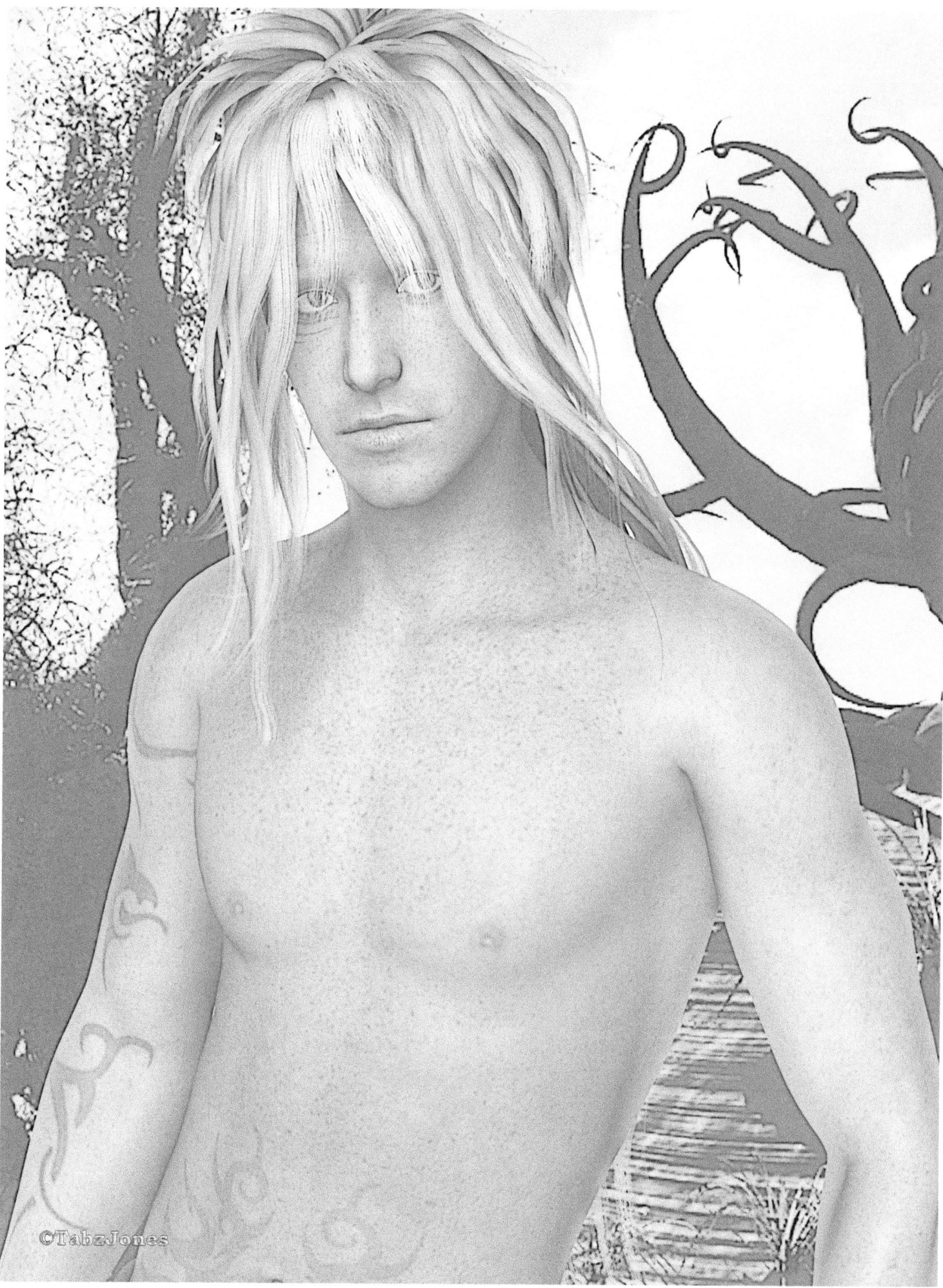
©TabzJones

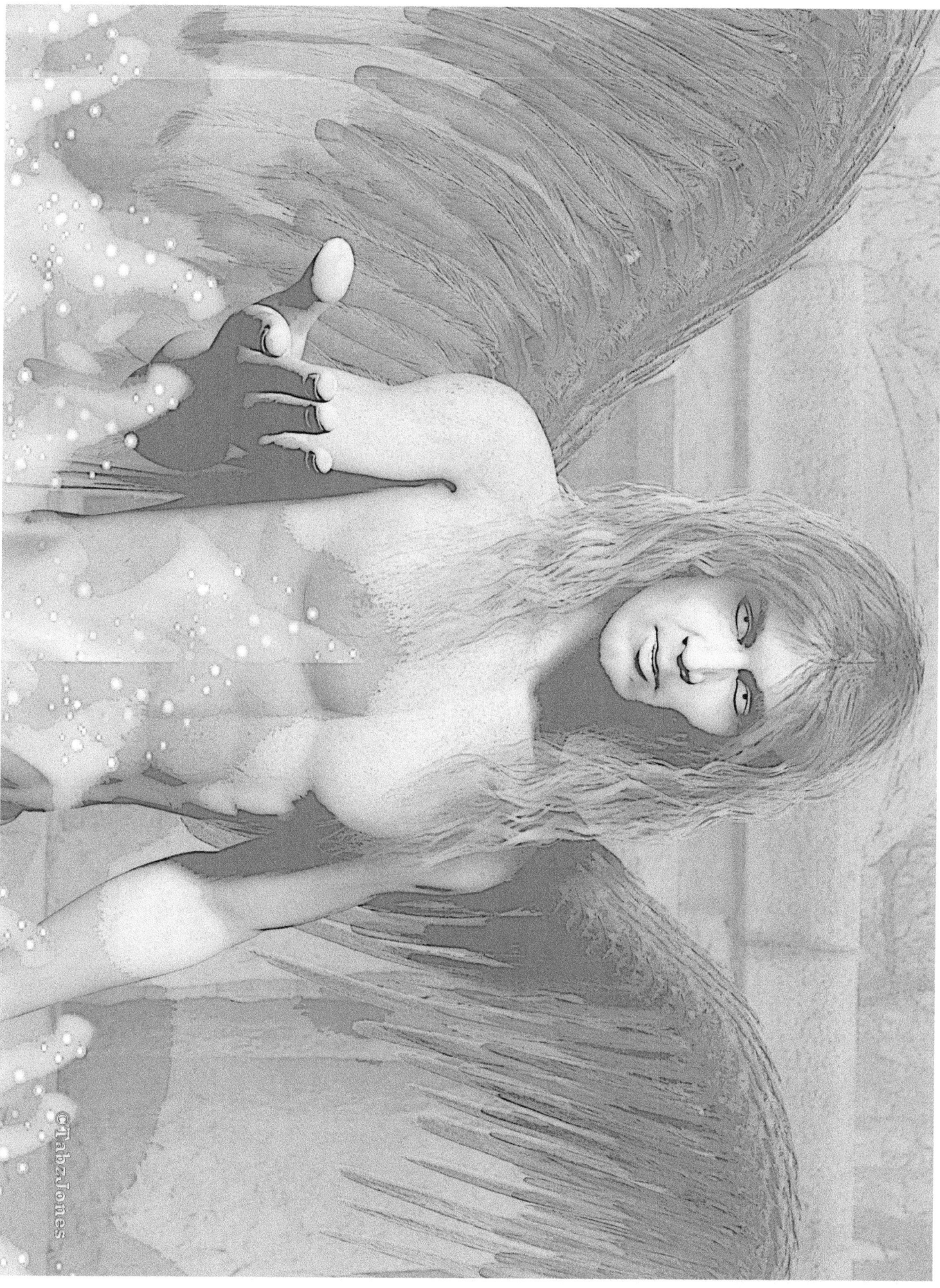

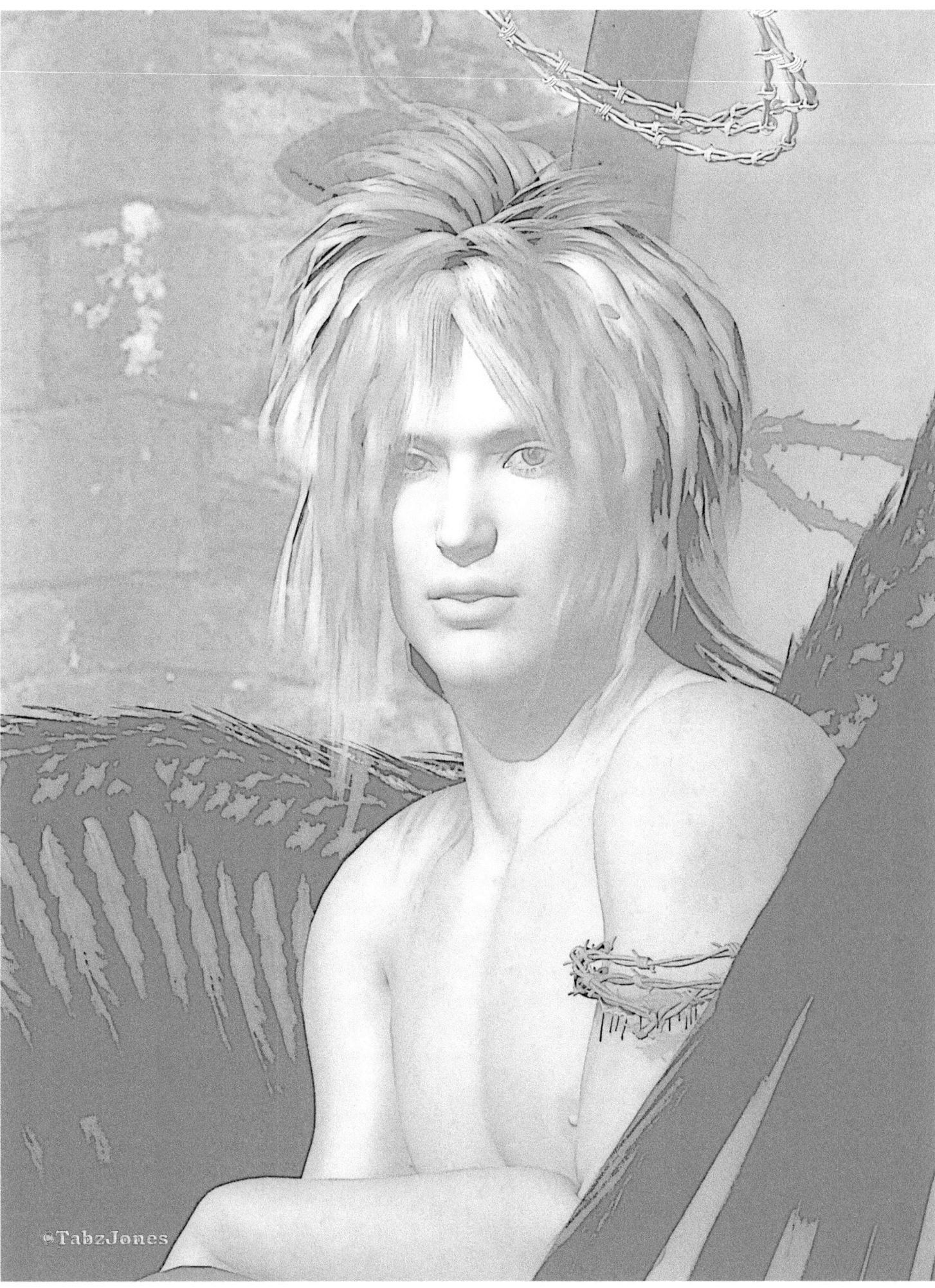

©TabzJones

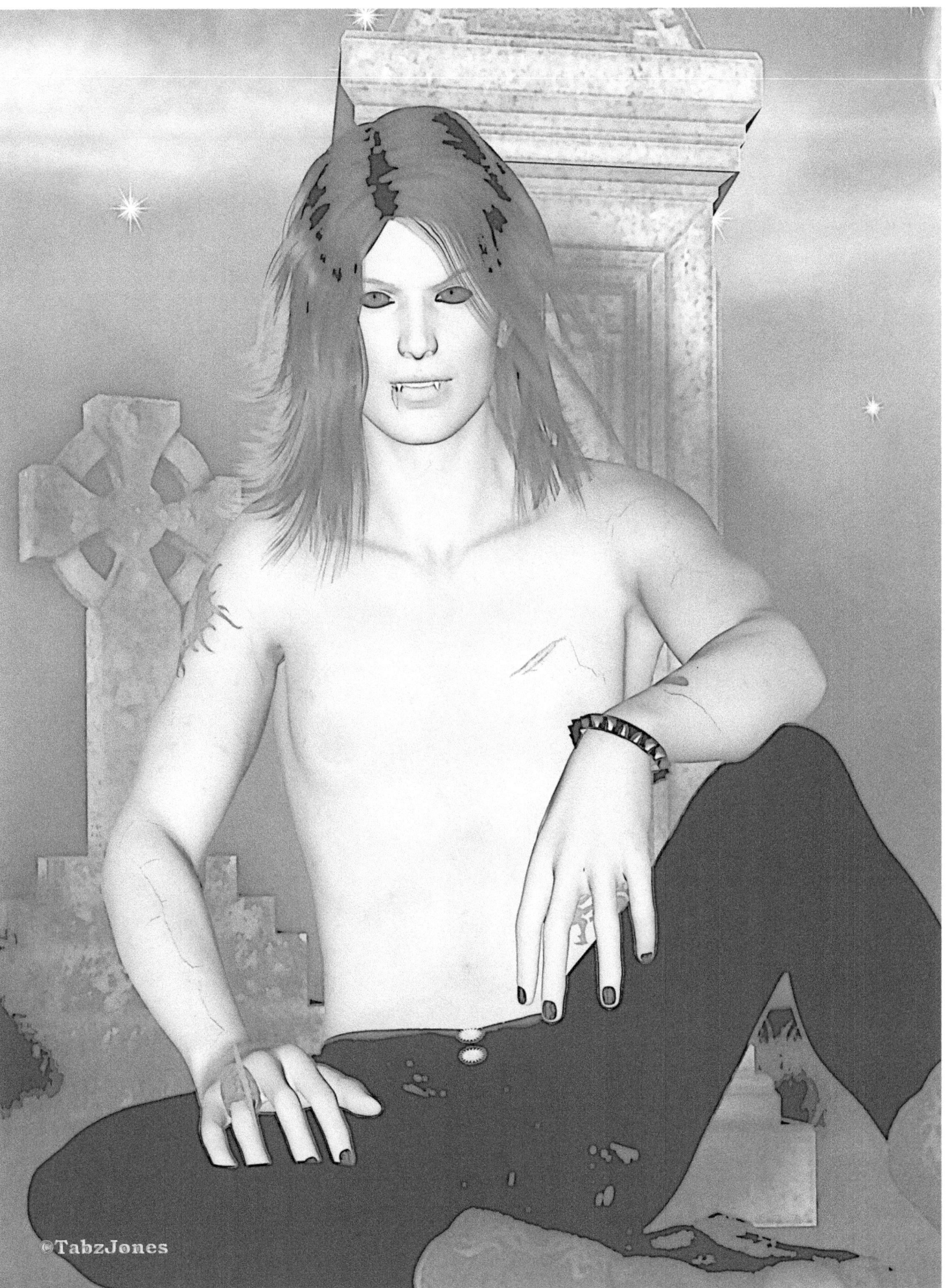

©TabzJones

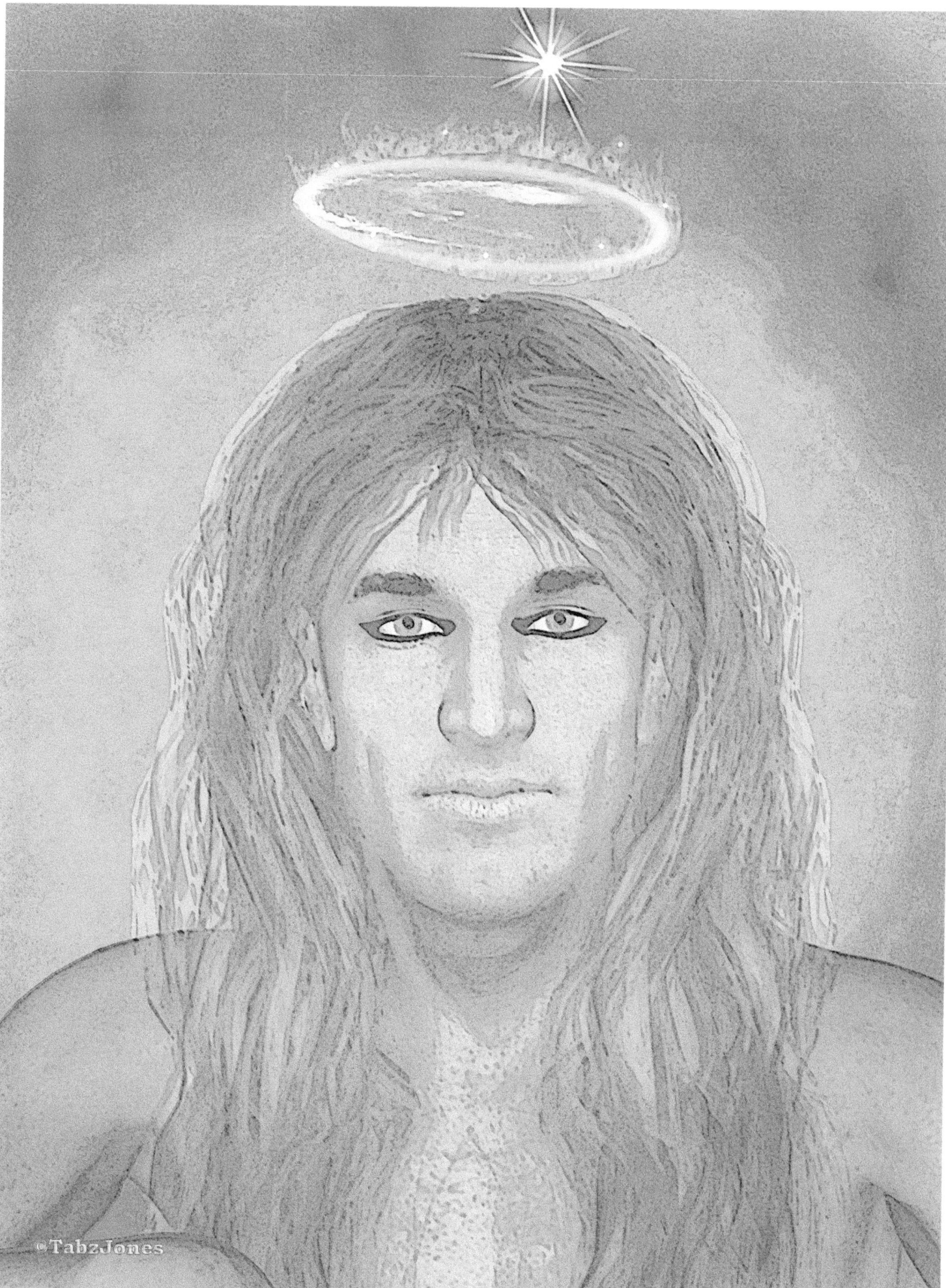

©TabzJones

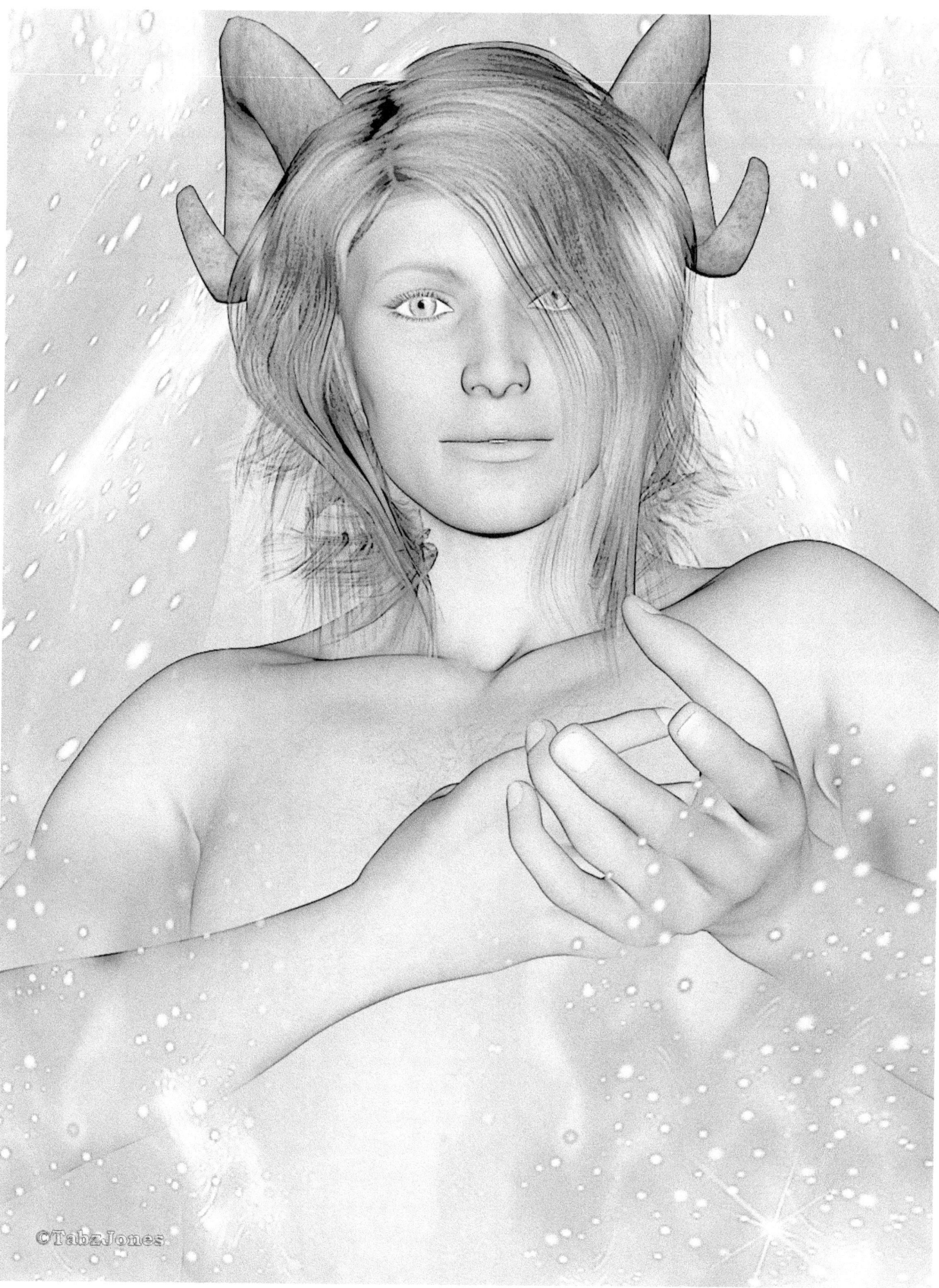
©TabzJones

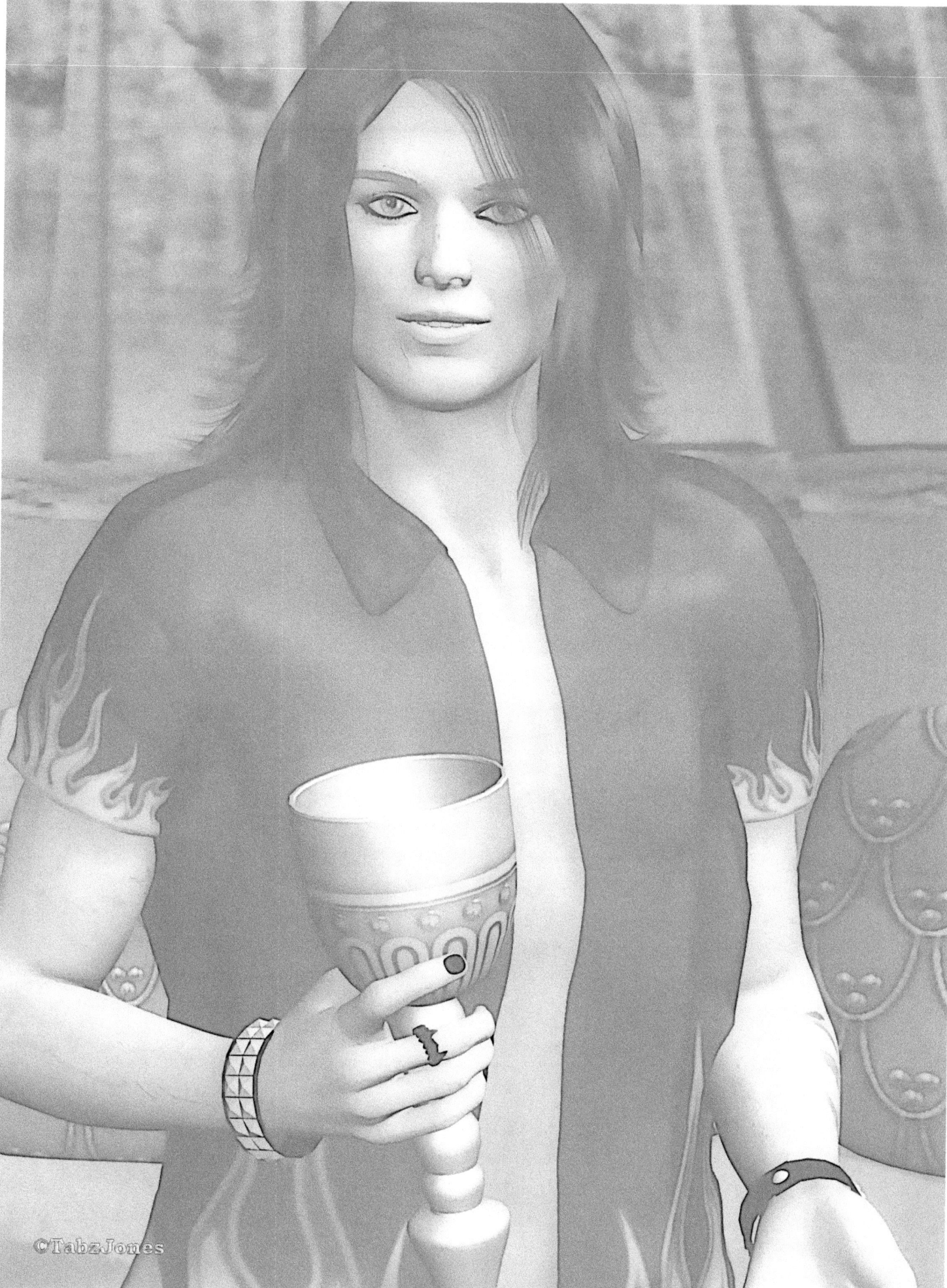

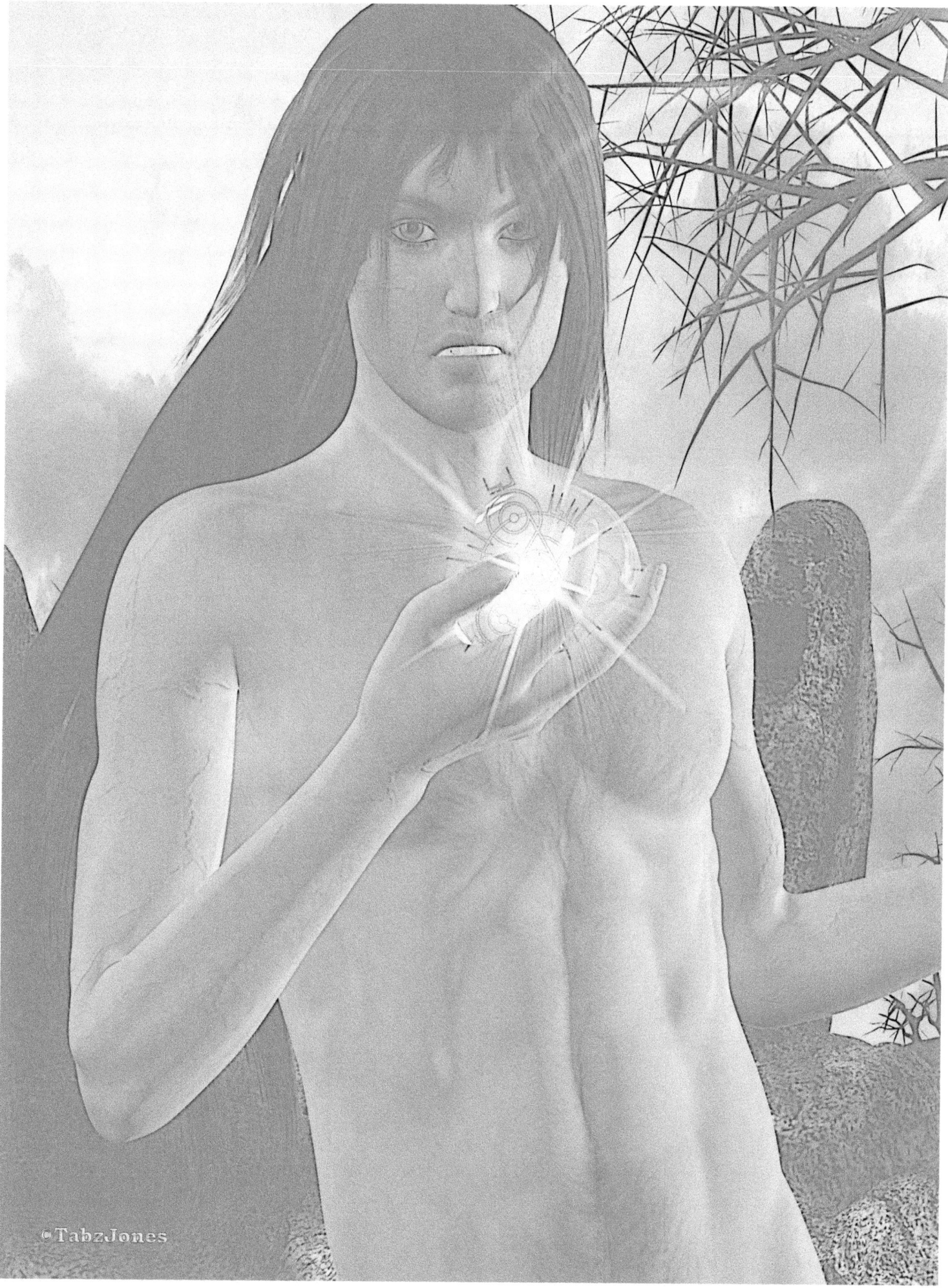

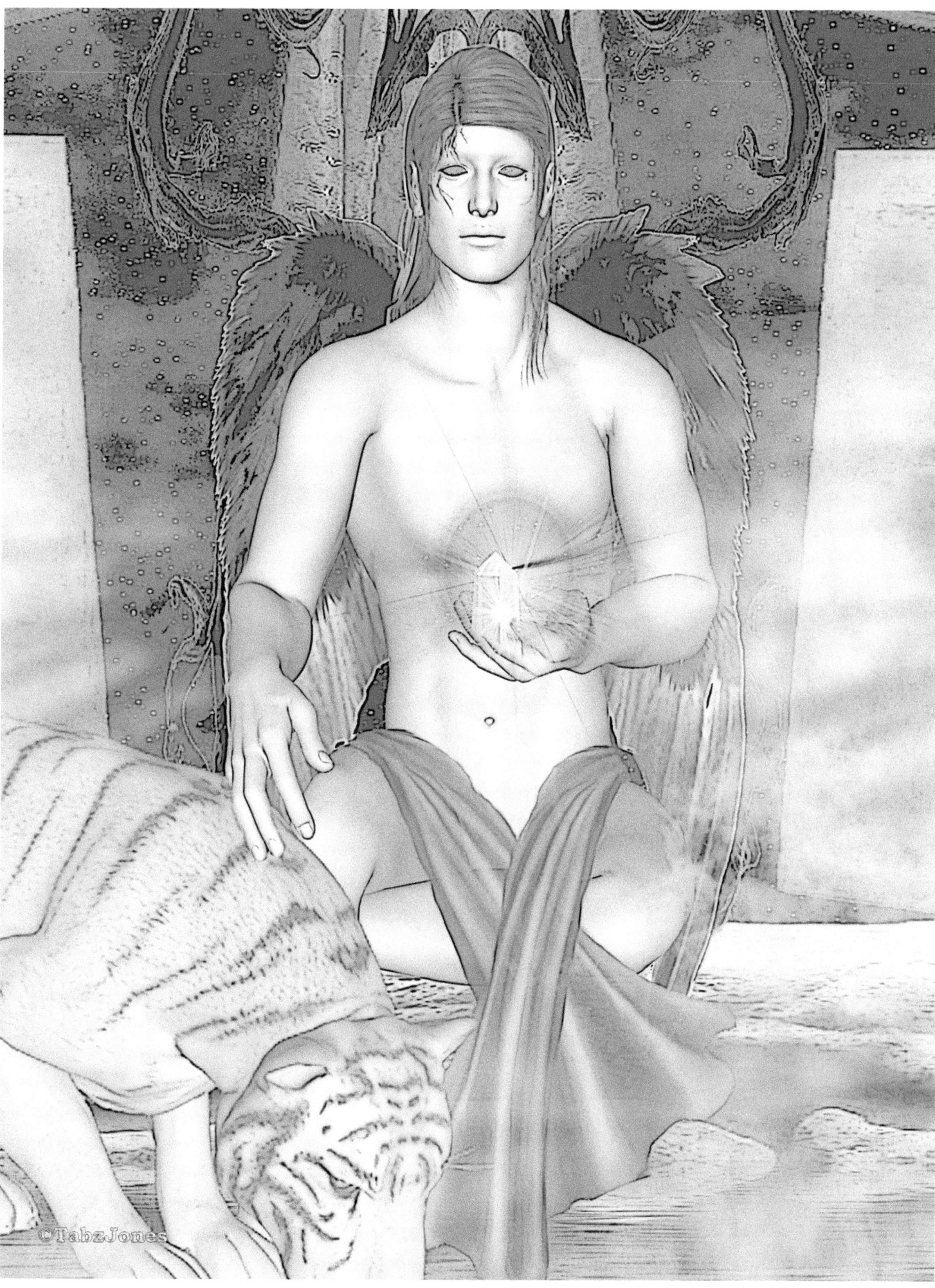

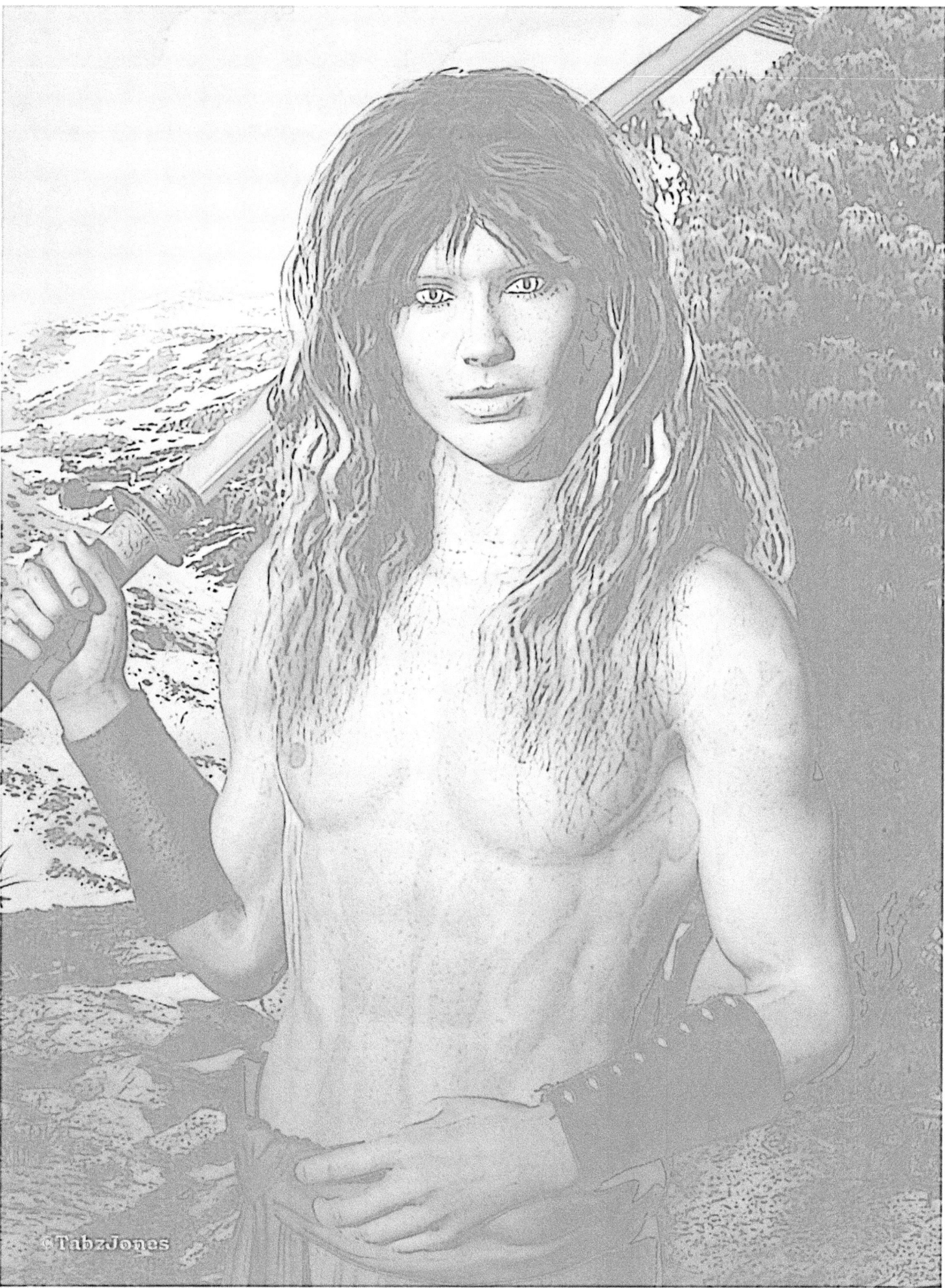
©TabzJones

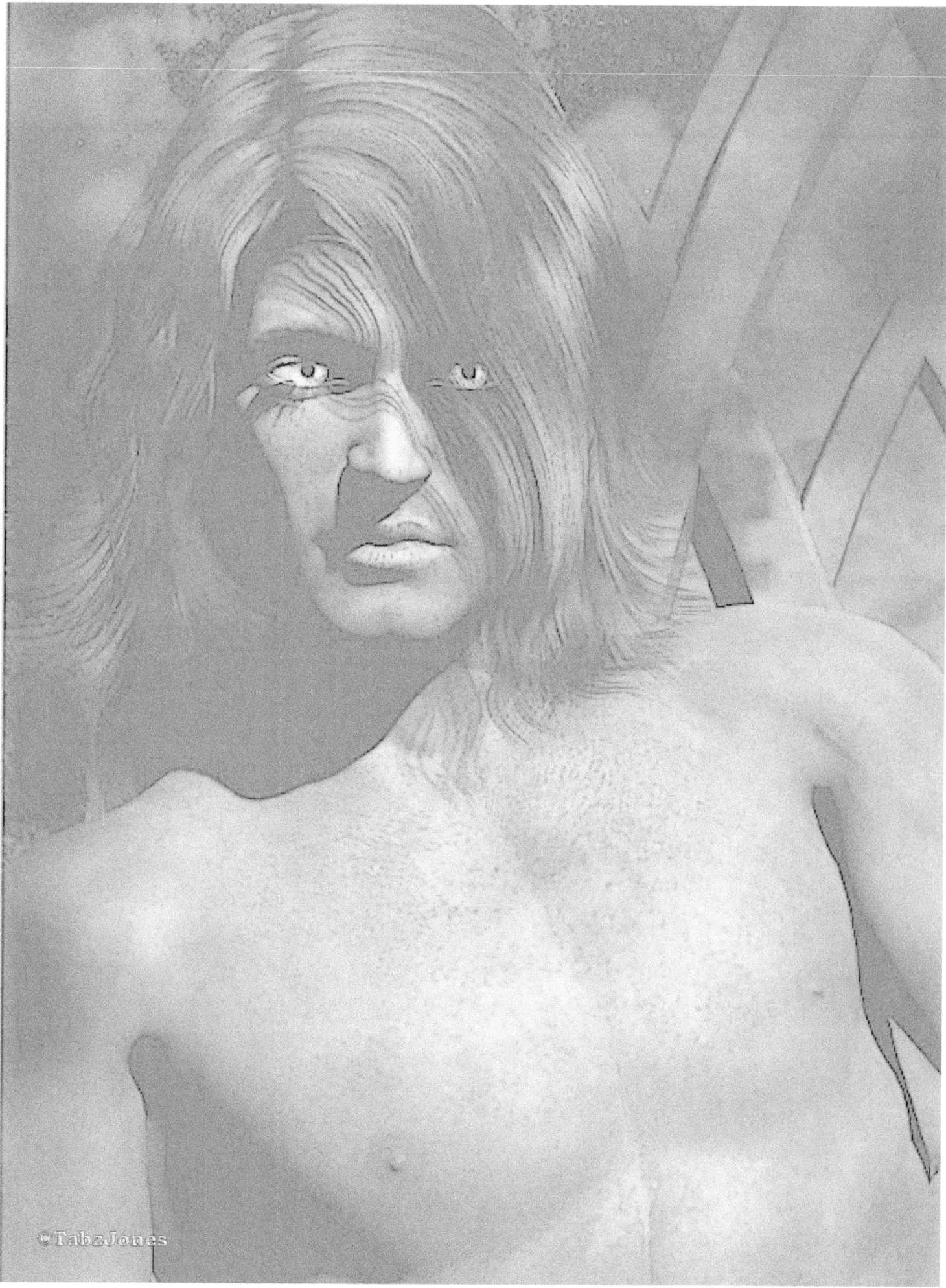

©TabzJones

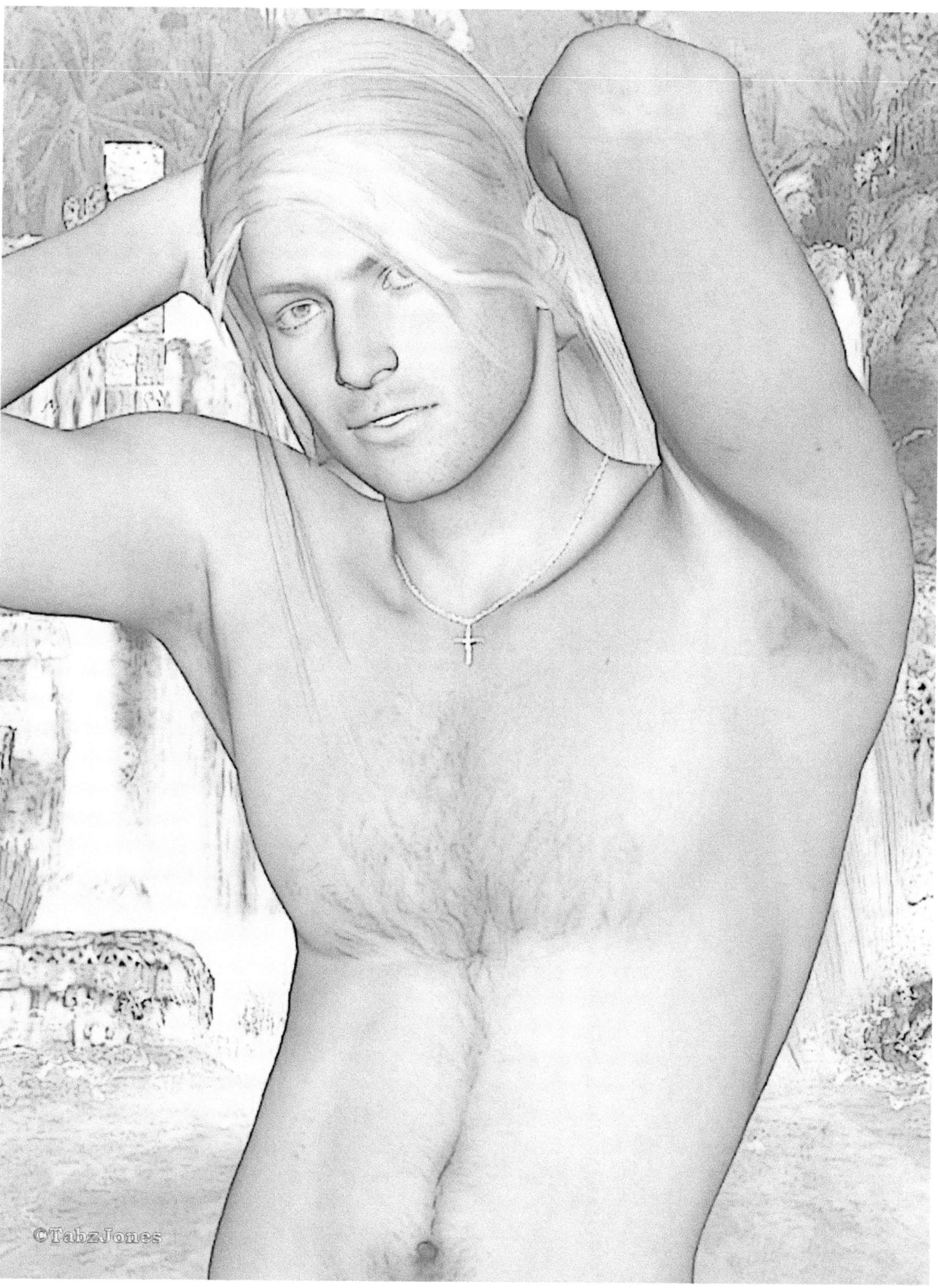
©TabzJones

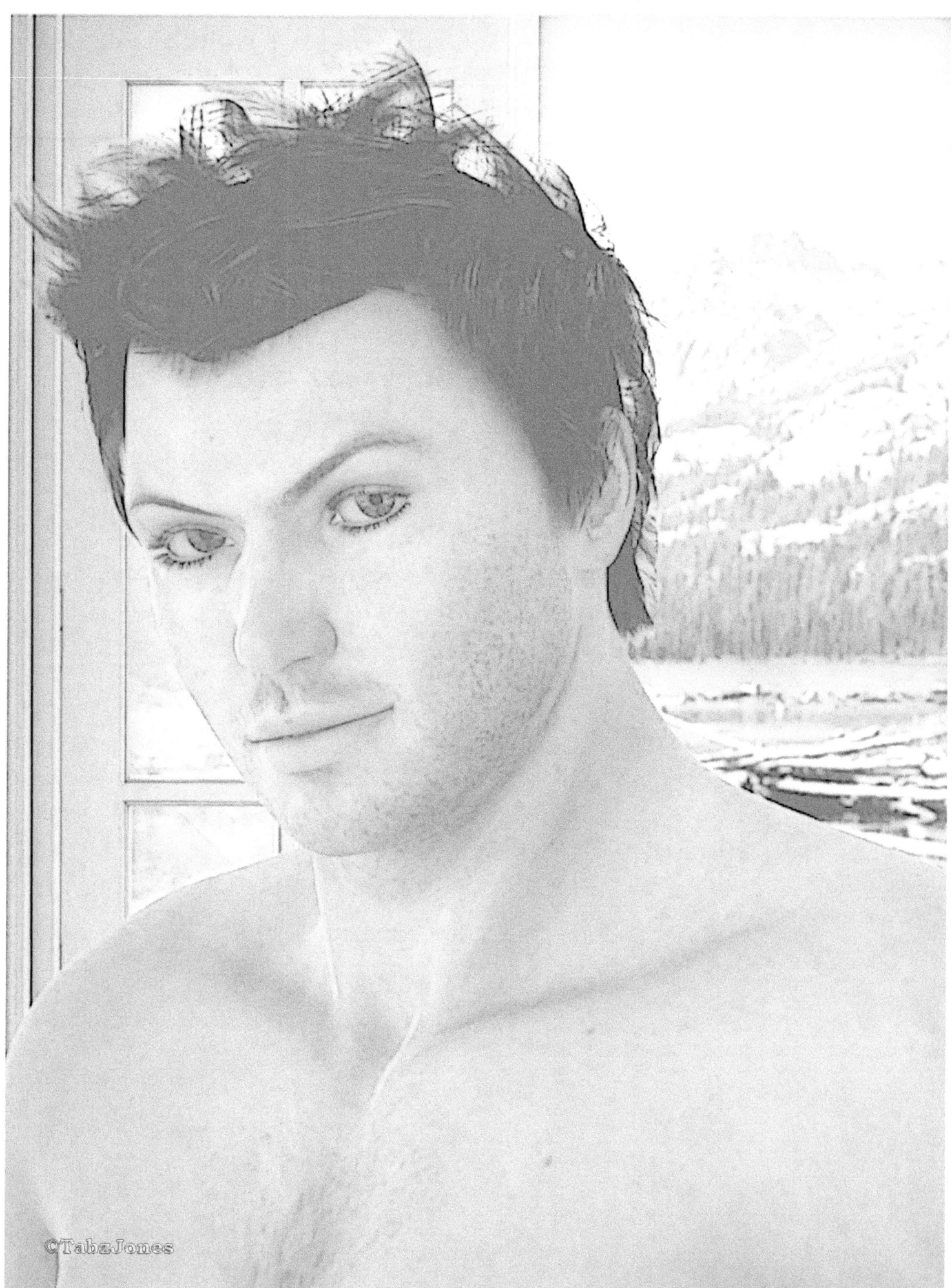

©TabzJones

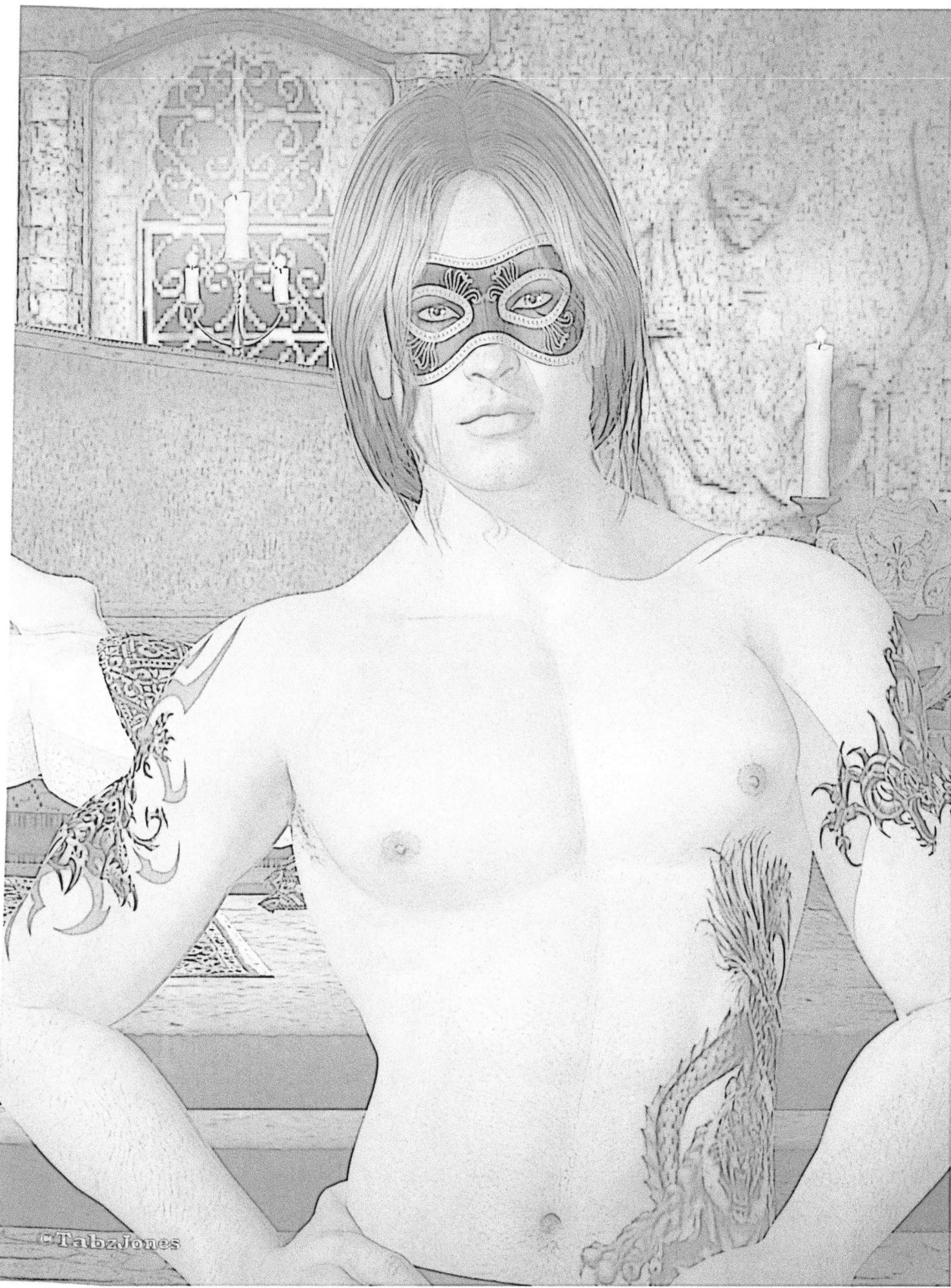

www.ingramcontent.com/pod-product-compliance
Lightning Source LLC
Chambersburg PA
CBHW080602190526
45169CB00007B/2851